Do They Exist?

Do Aliens Exist?

Stuart A. Kallen

ReferencePoint Press®

San Diego, CA

For more information, contact:
ReferencePoint Press, Inc.
PO Box 27779
San Diego, CA 92198
www.ReferencePointPress.com

LIBRARY OF CONGRESS CATALOGING-IN-PUBLICATION DATA

Kallen, Stuart A., 1955- author.
  Do aliens exist? / by Stuart A. Kallen.
    pages cm. -- (Do they exist?)
  Audience: Grades 9 to 12.
  Includes bibliographical references.
  ISBN-13: 978-1-60152-852-0 (hardback)
  ISBN-10: 1-60152-852-3 (hardback)
  1. Extraterrestrial beings--Juvenile literature. 2. Human-alien encounters--Juvenile literature.
  3. Life on other planets--Juvenile literature. I. Title.
  QB54.K34 2015
  001.942--dc23
                                                          2015021297

Contents

What Are Space Aliens?

A recent poll commissioned by the National Geographic Channel revealed some surprising views on the topic of space aliens. The poll found that 36 percent of American adults, or 80 million people, believe that space aliens are real. A similar percentage of the population believes that aliens have visited Earth. Additionally, one in ten respondents reports having personally seen an unidentified flying object, or UFO. Not everyone is as certain about the existence of extraterrestrial beings. Around 48 percent say they are not sure that aliens exist, and 17 percent say extraterrestrials definitely do not exist.

The widespread belief in aliens explains the countless websites, books, films, and television shows that speculate about the behavior and appearance of extraterrestrials. These sources describe common life-forms seen by those who claim to have encountered aliens. Tall, thin aliens are known as Tall Whites. Beautiful blond creatures that resemble angels are called Nordics. And giant lizard-like monsters are referred to as Reptoids or Reptilians.

The most common type of extraterrestrial, described in 90 percent of all North American encounters, is called a Grey (usually spelled with an *e* rather than with an *a*). Greys are short and hairless with long arms and three or four fingers. Grey aliens were popularized in the 1977 blockbuster film *Close Encounters of the Third Kind* and were later featured in several books about the alleged 1947 UFO crash near Roswell, New Mexico. Since that time Greys have been featured in movies, television programs, video games, graphic novels, and other media.

Searching for Evidence of Alien Life

Astronomers, physicists, and other scientists also frequently discuss alien life. But when the subject arises in papers and conferences, for instance, it becomes immediately clear that they are not talking about Greys, Reptoids, or any of the other beings that are commonly found in pop culture and personal accounts. In fact, few researchers believe aliens have ever visited Earth. However, most space scientists agree that there is a very high chance that other life-forms exist somewhere in the universe.

The US space agency, NASA, leads the way in the scientific exploration of alien worlds. In 2015 NASA introduced an initiative

People who claim to have been abducted by aliens give remarkably similar descriptions of their captors. They are often described as having short, hairless bodies; long, thin arms; grayish skin; and large round or oval eyes.

called Nexus for Exoplanet System Science (NExSS). The NExSS program assembled a team of scientists to determine whether alien life exists on exoplanets, or planets circling distant Sun-like stars. Astronomers believe that any one of the 40 billion Earth-like exoplanets in the universe might host alien life-forms. As NASA scientist Ellen Stofan said in 2015, "I think we're going to have strong indications of life beyond Earth within a decade, and I think we're going to have definitive evidence within 20 to 30 years."[1]

Trillions of Miles Away

Stofan and other scientists might very well be right about the existence of alien life somewhere among the countless planets in the universe. However, those planets are so far away that it is unlikely that even highly intelligent aliens could make the long interstellar journey to Earth. For example, the closest star to Earth, Alpha Centauri, is 24 trillion miles (38.6 trillion km) away. As Robert Todd Carroll, host of the Skeptic's Dictionary website, explains,

> Even traveling at one million miles an hour [1.6 million km/h], it would take more than 2,500 years to get there. To get there in twenty-five years would require traveling at more than 100 million miles an hour [160 million km/h] for the entire trip. Our fastest spacecraft, Voyager, travels at about 40,000 miles an hour [64,374 km/h] and would take 70,000 years to get to Alpha Centauri.[2]

Belief Is Real

Despite the enormous obstacles involved in space travel, millions of people continue to believe in extraterrestrials. Some have even considered how they would respond in the event of an alien visitation. Many of those polled—one in four Americans—say they would try to make friends with aliens if aliens ever visited Earth. Some respondents are less bold. Thirteen percent say they would lock themselves indoors if extraterrestrial beings landed on Earth. An even smaller percentage have decided they will not take any chances: 5 percent say they would try to kill the aliens.

The poll also revealed a strong distrust in government when it comes to alien visitations. An amazing eight out of ten Americans believe in government conspiracy theories purporting that NASA, the military, or some other official entity is hiding information about the existence of aliens from the public. Around 50 percent of the conspiracy theorists say men in black, or secret government agents who wear black suits, threaten people who claim to have seen aliens or UFOs.

A Big Jump

The belief in little gray men with big round eyes has been fueled by popular culture. Thousands of sources promote extraordinary theories about aliens. Some claim that aliens traveled to Earth long ago to construct the pyramids in Egypt, and others assert that extraterrestrials are conducting breeding experiments to create a hybrid human-alien race. One of the most enduring conspiracy theories is the idea that aliens have infiltrated the US government and control missiles, spacecraft, and nuclear weapons. These concerns are reinforced by science fiction movies, television shows, and Internet blogs.

> "There is probably . . . curious stuff in the atmosphere. The jump to the conclusion that it is alien life is a big jump and would require quite extraordinary proof."[3]
>
> —Chris McKay, NASA astrobiologist.

Conspiracy theorists are not the only ones making remarkable claims when it comes to space aliens. Thousands of ordinary citizens—and even well-known people such as former president Jimmy Carter and actor Russell Crowe—claim to have seen alien spaceships. When credible people make such claims, the temptation is to accept their statements as fact. NASA astrobiologist Chris McKay urges caution in drawing conclusions from these accounts: "There is probably . . . curious stuff in the atmosphere. The jump to the conclusion that it is alien life is a big jump and would require quite extraordinary proof."[3] So whatever the polls reveal about the American public, those who are skeptical about the existence of aliens will still require extraordinary proof before they start forming an extraterrestial welcoming committee.

Chapter 1

Why Do People Believe in Space Aliens?

> *"The vast bodies of the planets, having . . . many things in common with the earth, share with it in being inhabited."*
>
> —Pierre-Louis Moreau de Maupertuis, head of the Royal Prussian Academy of Sciences (1746–1759).
>
> Quoted in Michael J. Crowe, *The Extraterrestrial Life Debate, 1750–1900.* Cambridge, UK: Cambridge University Press, 1986, p. 128.

> *"Nowhere in all space or on a thousand worlds will there be men to share our loneliness. . . . Of men elsewhere, and beyond, there will be none forever."*
>
> —Loren Eiseley, anthropologist, philosopher, and natural scientist.
>
> Loren Eiseley, *Immense Journey.* New York: Random House, 1957, p. 162.

In 2013 NASA astrobiologist Stephan Freeland discussed the possibility of extraterrestrial life. Freeland posed two questions that people have asked for thousands of years: "Are we alone? If we're not alone, would other life look like us?"[4] These questions go beyond science; they address a common hope that humanity is not alone and isolated in the cold, dark reaches of outer space.

Whether motivated by loneliness or simple curiosity, religious leaders, philosophers, and ordinary people have debated the mystery of alien life for centuries. And there has almost always been a consensus that alien life does exist.

The belief is based on what is called the principle of plenitude, or abundance. Astronomy professor David A. Weintraub explains the principle:

> Once upon a time, 400 years ago, the wisest scholars in the western world knew, absolutely, that the universe was swarming with inhabited worlds, other Earths. The medieval doctrine of plenitude asserted that all of God's created worlds—the Sun, the Moon, the planets, the moons of Jupiter, the rings of Saturn, and all of the stars—must be inhabited. God, these scholars argued, had created these worlds and God always acts with purpose.[5]

The principle of plenitude also included all the stars that were said to have been created to provide warmth and light to living beings on the planets that orbited them.

Ancient Alien Beliefs

The roots of alien plenitude can be traced back to ancient Hindu texts called Vedas, dating to around 1700 BCE; the Vedas are among the oldest written documents in which descriptions of extraterrestrials appear. The Vedas refer to the universe as an ocean of space filled with uncountable planets called islands. In Vedic tradition there are four hundred thousand species of living beings in the universe that take human-like forms. Many of these species are far more advanced than humans. Hindu religious scholar C. Prabhupada describes aliens in one part of the universe: "The topmost planet is called Satyaloka, or Brahmaloka. Beings of the greatest talents live on this planet. The presiding deity of Brahmaloka is Brahma . . . a living being like so many of us, but he is the most talented personality in the material world."[6]

Centuries after the Vedas were written, scholars, mathematicians, and astronomers in Greece contemplated the idea of worlds that might exist unseen by human eyes. Writing around 250 BCE, the Greek philosopher Epicurus discussed the possibility of tiny particles, or atoms, forming the basis of all life on Earth—and on other worlds:

> There is an infinite number of worlds, some like this world, others unlike it. . . . For the atoms out of which a world might arise, or by which a world might be formed, have not all been expended on one world or a finite number of worlds, whether like or unlike this one. Hence there will be nothing to hinder an infinity of worlds. . . . Nobody can prove that in one sort of world there might not be contained . . . the seeds out of which animals and plants arise and all the rest of the things we see.[7]

For centuries scholars believed that all of the planets of the solar system were inhabited. They saw this as the work of God.

The idea of other worlds and the possibility of life developing on those worlds was disputed even in ancient Greece. Writing around 350 BCE, the Greek scientist and philosopher Aristotle stated that Earth sat at the center of the universe and the Sun, Moon, planets, and stars all orbited Earth. Knowing the universe cannot have two centers, Aristotle argued that "there cannot be more worlds than one."[8]

Life on Jupiter and the Moon

Aristotle's ideas about the Earth-centered universe dominated European thought for two thousand years. However, this changed in 1609 after Italian astronomer Galileo Galilei made improvements to the telescope that allowed him to observe nearby planets. Galileo came to understand that Earth and other planets revolved around the Sun, not the other way around.

Peering through his telescope, Galileo saw that the Moon was Earth-like with mountains, valleys, and craters. Galileo also studied Venus, gazed upon the rings of Saturn, and discovered four of Jupiter's sixty-seven moons. Galileo named the moons of Jupiter Europa, Io, Ganymede, and Callisto after mythical figures who were lovers of the Greek god Zeus (Jupiter in Roman mythology).

Galileo's findings initiated a four-centuries-long scientific debate over what was called cosmic pluralism. This is the belief that numerous, or plural, worlds exist beyond Earth and that these worlds most likely harbor alien life. German astronomer Johannes Kepler was a strong supporter of cosmic pluralism. Kepler wrote that if Earth's moon existed for the benefit of humans, the moons of Jupiter surely existed for a similar reason. He speculated it was to provide light at night for beings who populated the planet and its moons. In 1618 Kepler wrote,

> It is not improbable . . . that there are inhabitants not only on [Jupiter's moons], but on Jupiter too. Those four little moons exist for Jupiter, not for us. Each planet in turn, together with its occupants, is served by its own satellites. From this line of reasoning, we deduce with the highest degree of probability that Jupiter is inhabited.[9]

Inspired by Kepler, in 1638 British minister John Wilkins wrote a book titled *The Discovery of a World in the Moone, or, a Discourse Tending to Prove That 'Tis Probable There May Be Another Habitable World in That Planet*. In the book Wilkins writes, "Tis probable there may be inhabitants in this other World [the Moon], but of what kinde they are is uncertain. . . . The inhabitants of that world [the Moon] are not men as wee are, but some other kinde of creatures."[10] Wilkins speculated that these beings shared similar proportions and appearance with humans.

Throughout the seventeenth and eighteenth centuries, cosmic pluralism was an accepted possibility among astronomers, philosophers, and even politicians. Benjamin Franklin—a US founder, statesman, and scientist—believed in cosmic pluralism. As Franklin wrote in 1749, "It is the opinion of all the modern philosophers and mathematicians that the planets are inhabitable worlds."[11] He was not alone in this view. Pierre-Louis Moreau de Maupertuis, head of the Royal Prussian Academy of Sciences from 1746 to 1759, summed up the attitude of the day: "This planet [Earth] can convince us that all the others, which appear to be of the same nature as it, are not deserted globes suspended in the skies, but that they are inhabited."[12]

> "It is the opinion of all the modern philosophers and mathematicians that the planets are inhabitable worlds."[11]
>
> —Benjamin Franklin, author, scientist, inventor, and statesman.

Martian Canals

By the mid-nineteenth century, telescopes had improved enough to allow astronomers to observe in great detail the geological features of Mars. The respected Italian astronomer Giovanni Schiaparelli was fascinated with Mars and studied it regularly between 1877 and 1890. Schiaparelli discovered what he believed to be a network of gullies and canyons running across the Martian surface. He published numerous maps of Mars describing what he called *canali*. In Italian, the word *canali* refers to channels or grooves that are created by wind, water, or other natural forces. When translated into English, *canali* means "canals," a word that implies irrigation channels designed by intelligent beings for trans-

Life on Mars

Percival Lowell and Edward S. Morse believed that Mars had an Earth-like atmosphere that made Martian life possible. In fact, though, the atmosphere on Mars is one hundred times thinner than Earth's atmosphere, and it is 96 percent carbon dioxide (CO_2). Since CO_2 is unbreathable, animal life cannot exist on Mars. However, Morse's ideas about Mars were based on the most current information available in 1906 when he wrote the book *Mars and Its Mystery*, which speculates on the Earth-like characteristics of Mars:

> Recalling the resemblance which Mars bears to the Earth, and the data which have already been established, we behold a world in many respects like ours, with its sunsets and sunrises, winds that sweep over its surface, the dust storms from the deserts, its snowstorms and snow-drifts, its dazzling fields of white in the north, with an occasional snow-storm that whitens the planet far down in latitude; the seasonal changes, and, most important of all, the melting ice caps, with rivulets and torrents, temporary arctic seas and frozen pools, its great expanses of vegetation and sterile plains. We have in Mars the variety of conditions under which life has assumed its infinite variety of aspects on the Earth, and which, by analogy, should have passed through similar stages in Mars.

Edward S. Morse, *Mars and Its Mystery*. Boston: Little, Brown, 1906, p. 16.

porting water. When the press picked up on the story about canals on Mars, a wave of Martian mania swept through Europe and the United States.

One of the people caught up in the fervor was Percival Lowell, a wealthy amateur astronomer born in Boston in 1855. In 1892

Lowell set out to prove the existence of Martian canals. Using a portion of his family fortune, Lowell built the Lowell Observatory on a mountain outside the then small settlement of Flagstaff, Arizona. Perched at an elevation of 7,000 feet (2,134 m) above sea level, the Lowell Observatory features a 12-inch (30-cm) telescope. Today the Lowell Observatory telescope is mainly used by amateur astronomers, but when it was erected it was the most powerful telescope of the era.

Lowell spent countless hours in the chilly Arizona night peering up at Mars. Although his eyesight was failing, Lowell discovered that Mars was indeed like Earth in some respects. The planet, with its twenty-four-hour day, has raging dust storms and polar ice caps. Unknown to Lowell, the ice is made from carbon dioxide, not water. Nonetheless, he saw the ice generate drifting white clouds and even snowstorms. Lowell also believed Mars was latticed with a great network of canals.

Through his telescope, Percival Lowell saw what he believed to be a network of water canals on Mars. On this globe, made between 1903 and 1909, the lines signify the canals that—in Lowell's view—gave credence to the idea of an inhabited, Earth-like planet.

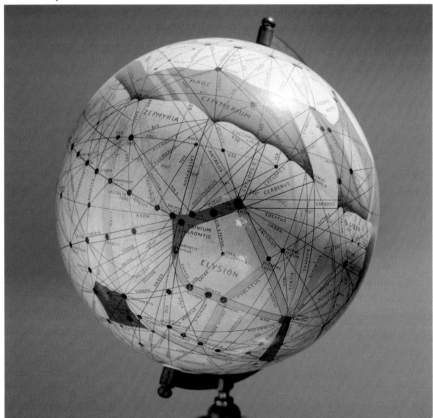

From his observations, Lowell deduced that the red surface of Mars was an arid desert little different than the one in Arizona. He wrongly believed the temperatures on Mars were about the same as southern England and incorrectly determined the Martian air was thin but there was enough oxygen to support life. Lowell believed that the canals moved melting water from the poles across the planet's equator. He also thought the canals were filled with an intelligent race of fish-like Martians that had survived for eons in the life-giving waters.

Vegetables and Vegetation

Lowell published his findings in the 1906 best-selling book *Mars and Its Canals*. The scientific theories Lowell put forth in the book convinced many people, including scientists, that Martians were real. Edward S. Morse, director of the prestigious Peabody Museum at Yale University, supported Lowell's idea of an Earth-like Mars with an atmosphere that supported life. Morse's book *Mars and Its Mystery* concluded that life on Mars evolved much as it had on Earth.

In Great Britain, scientist E.H. Hankin called Lowell brilliant and published an article in the scientific journal *Nature* supporting the idea of Martian life. In all seriousness Hankin wrote, "Perhaps on Mars there is only one living being, a gigantic vegetable the branches . . . of which embrace the planet like an octopus [and] suck water from the melting polar caps."[13]

While scientific authorities convinced the public that life existed on Mars, not all scholars agreed with the idea. A year after Lowell published his book, the British biologist Alfred Russel Wallace responded with his own book, *Is Mars Habitable?* Wallace wrote that Mars was so cold that any water would be frozen. As far as Lowell's canals went, Wallace was scathing: "Any attempt to make that scanty surplus [of water], by means of overflowing canals, travel across the equator into the opposite hemisphere, through such terrible desert regions . . . as Mr. Lowell describes, would be the work of a body of madmen rather than of intelligent beings."[14]

> "Perhaps on Mars there is only one living being, a gigantic vegetable the branches . . . of which embrace the planet like an octopus."[13]
>
> —E.H. Hankin, British scientist.

Playing on People's Fears

When the radio show version of *The War of the Worlds* was broadcast on Halloween night 1938, millions of people panicked, believing that Martians were invading Earth. Investigative journalist Annie Jacobsen explains why so many people were taken in by a radio play about an alien invasion:

> [The] *War of the Worlds* broadcast tapped into the nation's growing fears. Just two weeks before, Adolf Hitler's troops had invaded Czechoslovakia, leaving the security of Europe unclear. Rapid advances in science and technology, which included radar, jet engines, and microwaves, left many Depression-era Americans overwhelmed by how science might affect a coming war. Death rays and murderous Martians may have been pure science fiction in 1938 but the concepts played on people's fears of invasion and annihilation. Man has always been afraid of the sneak attack, which is exactly what Hitler had just done in Czechoslovakia and what Japan would soon accomplish at Pearl Harbor. The weapons introduced in World War II included rockets, drones, and the atomic bombs—[and] were all foreshadowed in Wells's story. Advances in science were about to fundamentally change the face of war and make science fiction not as fictional as it had once been.

Annie Jacobsen, *Area 51: An Uncensored History of America's Top Secret Military Base.* New York: Little, Brown, 2011, p. 21.

Wallace's theory about alien life received far less public attention than Lowell's fanciful theories about Martian fish creatures. Both books appeared during an era when long irrigation channels were being built in the United States and the French were trying to carve the Panama Canal across Central America. Astronomer and science communicator Carl Sagan explains how these massive building projects influenced attitudes at the time: "If Europeans and Americans could perform such feats, why not Martians? Might there not be an even more elaborate effort by an older and wiser species, courageously battling the advance of [the desert] on the red planet?"[15]

From Science Fiction to Science

By the time Lowell and others were speculating about Martians, extraterrestrials called Greys were already well known to readers of science fiction. Greys, or some variation of them, are short, hairless beings with scaly gray skin, bulbous heads, and elongated arms. The most recognizable feature of a Grey is its eyes, which are very large and black. The eyes wrap around, or slant, toward the back of the skull.

As early as 1891 Kenneth Folingsby described tiny gray alien men in the novel *Meda: A Tale of the Future.* The creatures had short legs and heads shaped like eggs. In *Meda* the gray extraterrestrials moved along like hot air balloons, floating down a country lane at what was then the amazing speed of 10 miles per hour (16 kph). Perhaps not surprisingly, several years after *Meda* was published newspapers in Boston, Sacramento, and elsewhere published reports from eyewitnesses who saw blimp-like UFOs with strange lights floating through the sky.

Greys were not the only type of aliens described in science fiction novels of the late nineteenth century. The 1898 classic *The War of the Worlds* by H.G. Wells portrays Martian invaders as horrid octopus-like monsters. They have numerous tentacle-like arms and disgusting, oily brown skin resembling fungus. Wells describes the appearance of the Martians as they emerged from their cylindrical spaceships in southern England: "The peculiar V-shaped mouth with its pointed upper lip, the absence of brow ridges, the absence of a chin beneath the wedgelike lower lip, the incessant quivering of this mouth. . . . Above all, the extraordinary intensity of the immense eyes—were at once vital, intense, inhuman, crippled and monstrous."[16]

Wells's Martians easily conquer England with weapons considered futuristic at the time. The aliens wage total war with robots, aerial bombings, and armored vehicles. A laser-like, bright green Heat-Ray liquefies metal, glass, and stone with its intense flames. Massive numbers of people are killed with a chemical weapon called black smoke discharged from rockets.

News of a Martian Invasion

In 1938 actor and producer Orson Welles turned *The War of the Worlds* into a radio show. On Halloween night a man claiming to be CBS reporter Carl Phillips told listeners he was on the scene in Grover's Mill, New Jersey, where a huge flaming object had crashed into a farm field. In a trembling voice Phillips announced, "The object doesn't look very much like a meteor. It looks more like a huge cylinder. The metal casing is definitely extraterrestrial!" Phillips began to scream: "Ladies and gentlemen, this is the most terrifying thing I have ever witnessed! Someone's crawling out of the hollow top!"[17] After Phillips described aliens using death rays to kill fifteen hundred people, another voice interrupted. A man claiming to be the secretary of the interior announced that an interplanetary war had begun and New York City was under mandatory evacuation.

The public reaction to *The War of the Worlds* shows that millions of people easily could be convinced that aliens were real. The broadcast caused thousands of people to run from their homes with wet towels over their faces to protect themselves against a Martian gas attack. In New York, New Jersey, and Canada, people jumped in their cars with their entire families and tried to flee the Martian invasion. Highway traffic was slowed to a crawl.

The mass hysteria was enough to warrant the attention of the US military. After the broadcast an unnamed military official told the Associated Press, "What struck the military . . . most about the radio play was its immediate emotional effect. Thousands of persons believed a real invasion had been unleashed. They exhibited all the symptoms of fear, panic, determination to resist, desperation, bravery, excitement or fatalism that real war would have produced."[18]

A Government Investigation

The public concern over aliens only increased after the *War of the Worlds* broadcast. By the late 1940s, newspapers and magazines were filled with eyewitness reports about mysterious flying saucers, unearthly alien wreckage, and humanoid extraterrestrials. A Gallup poll taken in 1950 revealed that 90 percent of Americans had heard of space aliens and flying saucers.

By 1952 the government was receiving so many reports about aliens and spaceships that the US Air Force launched an investigation called Project Blue Book. The rationale for Project Blue Book was to determine whether aliens were a threat to national security. While the Air Force was skeptical, Harvard astrophysicist J. Allen Hynek, who worked on the official investigation, concluded that one-third of UFO sightings could not be explained. By the time Project Blue Book ended in 1969, it contained twelve thousand reports of UFO sightings.

The very fact that the Air Force created Project Blue Book served to reinforce the widespread belief in aliens. Many also concluded that the government was covering up proof of alien existence. And as public interest climbed, the media published numerous reports about aliens. Even *Life*, the most popular magazine in the country, helped spread the idea that aliens were real. On April 7, 1952, *Life* published a sixteen-page cover story titled "There Is a Case for Interplanetary Saucers." The story began with the following: "The Air Force is now ready to concede that many saucer and fireball sightings still defy explanation; LIFE offers some scientific evidence that there is a real case for interplanetary saucers."[19]

Close Encounters with Aliens

While *Life* speculated about saucers and fireballs, Hollywood filmmakers realized there was money to be made exploiting people's fears of invasion and war. Throughout the 1950s and 1960s space aliens were brought to life in hundreds of science fiction movies. Though the plots revolved around invasions from outer space, many of these films were actually expressing widespread anxiety about the destruction of humanity by atomic bombs and nuclear radiation.

The Day the Earth Stood Still, a film released in 1951, features a typical doomsday theme of the era. The movie begins with a benevolent humanoid alien named Klaatu and his robot companion,

The Cold War fueled fears of war and nuclear destruction. Hollywood movies capitalized on those fears by creating hundreds of alien invasion movies—among them The Day the Earth Stood Still.

Gort, landing their spaceship in Washington, DC. Klaatu wants to warn the president that aliens of other planets are worried about the development of atomic power on Earth. Klaatu says that the human race will be eliminated if it does not stop building nuclear weapons.

The Day the Earth Stood Still was a low-budget film that might seem trite by modern standards, but it had a psychological effect on viewers. This film and others like it gave audiences a way to deal with their fears by merging the routines of daily living with the unthinkable prospect of nuclear annihilation. As writer and film critic Susan Sontag explained in a 1965 article, "We live under continual threat of two equally fearful, but seemingly opposed, destinies: unremitting banality and inconceivable terror."[20] Movies created a sense of normalcy even in the most unimaginable of circumstances.

Space alien films appeal to audiences for another reason: millions of people worldwide claim to have actually seen a UFO. Film director Steven Spielberg understood this when he featured kindhearted Greys in two blockbuster films: *Close Encounters of the Third Kind* (1977) and *E.T. the Extra-Terrestrial* (1982). In 1977 Spielberg discussed the inspiration for the making of *Close Encounters*:

> "I began meeting people who had had close encounters [with aliens] . . . where undeniably something quite phenomenal was happening right before their eyes."[21]
>
> —*Steven Spielberg, film director.*

I realized that just about every fifth person I talked to had looked up at the sky at some point in their lives and seen something that was not easy to explain. And then I began meeting people who had had close encounters [with aliens] . . . where undeniably something quite phenomenal was happening right before their eyes. . . . That got me interested in making the movie.[21]

Today humanoid aliens, both friendly and destructive, are regularly featured in films. Between 2011 and 2015, extraterrestrials appeared in at least forty-five major films and numerous alien races were expected to appear in new episodes of both the *Star Wars* and *Star Trek* series. Other offerings included *Outpost 37*, which follows a group of soldiers ten years after an alien invasion, and *Jupiter Ascending*, in which a young woman discovers her destiny as an heiress of intergalactic nobility. These films, with their stunning computer-generated graphics, produce vivid visions of extraterrestrial beings.

Greys and other alien life are also well represented on the Internet. Countless websites claim to have proof of the existence of extraterrestrials. They post documents that they identify as secret government reports and photos and videos of aliens and UFOs. Many websites are run by ufologists, researchers who contend that aliens have been visiting Earth for millennia.

> "People simply love to believe in weird things just because it's fun."[23]
>
> — *Ray Villard, journalist.*

Some say aliens have come to Earth to help humanity solve problems such as pollution, the threat of nuclear war, and global warming. Others believe aliens have supplied the US government with superior technology, including computers, lasers, and futuristic weapons. In exchange, the government hides the existence of aliens from the general public and builds fabulous underground cities for these mysterious beings. Darker conspiracy theories purport that the government supplies human beings to aliens for use in nefarious experiments.

"Because It's Fun"

With major media outlets, the military, and leading scientists all claiming (at various times) that aliens exist, it is little wonder that millions of people believe in extraterrestrials. For Michael Shermer of the *Skeptical Inquirer*, something called confirmation bias explains this widespread belief: "People tend to seek or interpret evidence favorable to their existing beliefs and ignore or misconstrue evidence unfavorable to those beliefs."[22] For example, two people might see a bright blob of light in the sky. Someone who believes in alien life-forms might think the light is a UFO piloted by Greys. A nonbeliever will attribute the same light to a military aircraft. Each person's bias confirms his or her belief.

Journalist Ray Villard has another thought about why so many people accept the notion that aliens exist on other worlds: "People simply love to believe in weird things just because it's fun."[23]

Chapter 2

Encounters with Aliens

"The majority of [alien] abductees do not appear to be deluded . . . lying, self-dramatizing, or suffering from a clear mental illness."

—John Mack, psychologist and professor at Harvard Medical School.

John Mack, "The Alien Abduction Phenomenon," UFO Evidence, 2011. www.ufoevidence.org.

"There simply is no scientifically credible evidence that we have alien visitors. . . . We've had more than 50 years to come up with artifacts, with evidence. And nobody has been able to come up with it."

—Philip Klass, alien researcher and skeptic.

Quoted in *Nova*, "Interview with Philip Klass," PBS, 1996. www.pbs.org.

Polls taken by major news and polling organizations over the last decade consistently reveal that about 8 million Americans, or 2.5 percent of the US population, believe they have been abducted by aliens. Many of the encounters sound strangely similar. The experiences often begin when the abductees (or contactees) are lying in bed or driving down a lonely highway in the dark of night. Suddenly they hear a deafening hum or grating metallic sound and mysterious flashing lights obscure their vision. They feel paralyzed while at the same time they experience a sensation of being transported into a spaceship through a wall, roof, windshield, or other solid surface.

Once inside the alien craft, abductees report seeing complex machines, flashing lights, and strange medical equipment. Gray-skinned aliens with spindly legs, pear-shaped heads, and big tear-shaped eyes rush about performing mysterious tasks while ignoring the abductee. Sometimes other humans are present. The aliens appear to be communicating through mental telepathy.

Many abduction experiences are reported as taking place in a medical examining room where the abductee is stripped of clothing. Bodily orifices are poked and probed. Sometimes a tiny metal chip is implanted in the brain, eye, ear, or other body part, leaving a strange scar. A surprising number of people report engaging in sex with aliens to produce hybrid human-alien beings.

The 1968 case of a young woman named Shane Kurz is typical of those who believe they were selected for breeding experiments. Kurz recalled under hypnosis that she was pulled up into an oval-shaped flying saucer by a beam of light. She was taken to a hospital-like room aboard the craft and was approached by an alien in a long white lab coat. The alien told Kurz she was a good breeder, then pushed a long needle into her navel and removed it. Another alien told Kurz telepathically that he was the leader, she was to have his baby, and she would remember nothing of the experience afterward. However, the breeding experiment seems to have failed because Kurz produced no hybrid human-alien baby.

Twin Abductees

Many abductees believe they have been picked up by aliens numerous times over the course of many years. Such was the case, first reported in 2009, by twins Audrey and Debbie. They were members of an alien awareness support group called Starborn, which claims fifteen hundred members. (Audrey and Debbie, like many abductees, withhold their last names and hometowns to avoid public ridicule.)

Audrey's and Debbie's alien encounters began when they were young. Audrey explains what she experienced: "I was probably about 5 years old or so and a bright blue light would come into the room and the door would open, and there would be like, a foggy kind of misty blue light, just shining through the whole

Many abductees have described being whisked from their homes or cars into hospital-like settings, where mysterious beings in white lab coats conduct experiments on their human subjects. Often, the aliens are also described as communicating telepathically.

house. And these two figures would come in. There would be a tall one, they had black capes, but they were bald and had big eyes."[24] While the young girls called their alien visitors the Bald Men, they fit the description of Greys provided by thousands of purported abductees.

The twins say the alien encounters continued over the years, with each being transported separately to spaceships. They were able to compare their experiences after each encounter. Audrey

"Have You Been Abducted by Aliens?"

In 2012 Harvard psychology professor Richard J. McNally and psychologist Susan Clancy conducted experiments with people who claimed to have been abducted by aliens. Subjects were recruited through a classified ad in the *Boston Globe* that asked, "Have you been abducted by aliens?" McNally describes those who responded to the ad:

> One man left a message nearly every night for about two weeks, consisting of him making strange noises ("Eeek, onk, blip, bleep") amounting to his rendition of an extraterrestrial language. Despite such inauspicious [unfavorable] beginnings, we did manage to recruit enough "real" abductees to complete our research. . . .
>
> One group comprised adults who reported "memories" of extraterrestrial kidnapping, whereas a second group reported a history of alien abduction, but had no . . . memories of the experience. These participants inferred abduction from diverse indicators such as mysterious marks on their bodies, panic attacks triggered by seeing pictures of the movie character E.T., and an inexplicable passion for reading science fiction. When Susan asked them what happened to their memories, they [speculated] that the aliens had zapped the memories from their brains or that the abduction had occurred in "another dimension."

Richard J. McNally, "Explaining 'Memories' of Space Alien Abduction and Past Lives: An Experimental Psychopathology Approach," Harvard University, May 13, 2015. http://dash.harvard.edu.

describes their impressions: "We have been up in crafts and seen our house from above. So we realized they are not from here. They are very good at mind erasing or whatever you want to call it. They'll leave you with bits and pieces of things you can remember. So we do remember certain things of being there together."[25]

The abductions were not pleasant, and the sisters experienced long-lasting trauma from the events. Audrey said the experience had greatly impacted her life and she had spent many years in therapy. As Debbie put it, "A lot of times I'll wake up in tears saying, 'Why me? Why me? Why can't this happen to somebody else.'"[26]

Intergalactic Breeding

The lives of many contactees take a turn for the weird after they publicize their alien encounters. This happened to Terrell Copeland, a former marine from Suffolk, Virginia. In 2005 Copeland was twenty-three years old. He was coming home from his night shift job as a forklift operator when he saw a massive triangular UFO floating over a Suffolk shopping center. Copeland was among several people who reported the sighting to a local newspaper.

Two years later Copeland had another close encounter with aliens. He saw a large orb of bouncing light pulsating in different colors floating 300 feet (91 m) above the ground in front of his apartment. Although Copeland was frightened, he was able to capture a video of the orb with his cell phone camera and posted it on YouTube. Soon after, a mysterious stranger knocked on his front door. When Copeland did not answer, the stranger scratched at the door and tried to turn the doorknob.

Copeland was dozing in a chair at the time and attempted to grab a gun he kept nearby. But he was paralyzed and could only move his eyes. A voice from outside told Copeland he did not need a gun, and he would not be harmed. Copeland said the man then identified himself as a military contractor and asked him if he "was ready for the truth," stating that the government has a "personal relationship with ET."[27]

The man left, but Copeland began experiencing another common symptom of alien encounters called missing time. During the following two nights, Copeland said he was not asleep but four hours seemed to have vanished. When he regained consciousness, he was aware but temporarily paralyzed. Copeland began keeping a log and writing down his vaguely remembered experiences during the missing time periods. He described one episode: "I was in a room and I saw a woman who did not have complete human features. She had the typical black eyes that you hear about. She had an elongated skull. And that startled me. And the next memory I have is me standing on my balcony waving at this cylinder-shaped ship."[28]

After Copeland told his story to Norfolk's *Virginian-Pilot* newspaper, he was approached by producers of a television show called *UFO Hunters*. After hearing Copeland's story, show host Bill Birnes declared Copeland to be a hybrid—a creature produced through intergalactic breeding who is being prepared for direct contact with his alien relatives. After appearing on the show, Copeland told a reporter that he agreed with Birnes and that he was waiting to meet the biological space entity who was his parent. When Copeland's mother was told that her son is part human and part alien, she was not shocked. As Copeland said, "I expected her to lose it but she didn't. She said there was always something strange about me."[29]

> "I was in a room and I saw a woman who did not have complete human features. She had the typical black eyes that you hear about. She had an elongated skull. And that startled me."[28]
>
> — *Terrell Copeland, alien contactee.*

Area 51

Most people who say they have encountered aliens have vague, dream-like memories of the experience. Photographs and videos of the purported visitations always seem to be blurry, and audio recordings are garbled. But some believe these isolated encounters are part of a larger pattern of alien visitations well known to the US government. And some ufologists claim that aliens have not only visited Earth but also actively work with military officials. This activity is said to occur in a place called Area 51, a restricted US Air Force facility in Nevada located 90 miles (145 km) northwest of Las Vegas.

Although the military has long refused to reveal the top secret activities that take place at Area 51, historical evidence shows that the facility is used to test experimental weapons and aircraft such as the F-117 fighter jet. Area 51 is a no-fly zone for commercial jets and is off-limits to civilians. Because of the secretive nature of Area 51 activities, the facility has played a central role in alien and UFO conspiracy theories since the 1970s.

Dozens of books and web pages written by ufologists claim crashed alien spacecraft are stored in Area 51 along with the bodies of dead aliens. Some say live aliens inhabit underground bunkers in Area 51, and they have worked with the US government to manufacture aircraft based on alien technology. The more bizarre conspiracy theories involve aliens working with scientists and military planners to control the weather, develop time-travel technology, or establish a world government to enslave humanity.

Area 51, a restricted US Air Force facility in Nevada, has long been the subject of rumor and speculation. The facility is at the center of the many alien and UFO conspiracy theories.

Aliens from Quintumnia

Claims about Area 51, made by Boyd Bushman in a 2014 You-Tube video, attracted a great deal of attention among ufologists. Bushman had worked as a senior scientist for the aerospace and defense company Lockheed Martin. He had helped create GPS devices and laser-guided smart bombs and held twenty-seven patents registered with the US Patent and Trademark Office.

Bushman was seventy-eight years old when he made a thirty-three-minute video shortly before his death on August 7, 2014. In the video, shot by another aerospace engineer, Bushman explains that for many years he had top secret clearance to work in Area 51. He claims he met eighteen aliens at the facility. They came from a planet called Quintumnia located sixty-eight light-years from Earth. Although sixty-eight light-years equals about 408 trillion miles (657 trillion km), the aliens were able to make the journey to Earth in forty-five minutes by using advanced technology.

> "They're able to use their own voice by telepathy to talk to you. You walk in the room with one of them, and all of a sudden you find yourself giving the answer to [their] question in your own voice."[30]
>
> —Boyd Bushman, aerospace scientist.

Like aliens in many encounter stories, those described by Bushman communicated without speaking: "They're able to use their own voice by telepathy to talk to you. You walk in the room with one of them, and all of a sudden you find yourself giving the answer to [their] question in your own voice."[30] Bushman said the aliens were humanoid, around 5 feet (1.5 m) tall with three backbones. He said they had ten webbed toes and ten fingers, which were 30 percent longer than those of an adult human. Some aliens lived as long as 230 years. Bushman divided the aliens into two groups, which he called wranglers and rustlers: "The two groups act differently. The ones that are wranglers are much more friendly, and have a better relationship with us."[31]

A Deathbed Prank?

According to Bushman, American engineers work with the aliens twenty-four hours a day. They are trying to reverse engineer

Symptoms of Alien Abduction

Joy S. Gilbert says she has been contacted by alien beings numerous times throughout her life. Gilbert's website, Alien Contact & Human Evolution, provides a number of symptoms experienced by alien abductees:

- Not feeling connected to your family here, of perceived origin. This causes a great deal of confusion.
- Feeling as if you come from someplace else, "out there." This is the feeling that somehow you have been left here without remembering why or by who.
- Often looking to the stars for answers you know somehow are there. . . .
- Recognizing yourself as being different from others! Actually this is quite a common experience for everyone on this planet, it seems. But Experiencers seem to feel it with greater intensity. . . .
- You do not tolerate living in large cities or being around numbers of people. People who experience [high] levels of consciousness and awareness [after meeting aliens] have a very sensitive Nervous System and their bodies react to environments that are overrun with people's thoughts and energies.
- Knowing things that cannot be proven, but you absolutely know them to be true.
- Seeing inter-dimensional beings as a young child, like angels, deceased family members and other beings.

Joy S. Gilbert, "Symptoms Alien Abduction," Alien Contact & Human Evolution, 2012. http://aliencontactandhumanevolution.com.

Quintumnian technology, taking apart spaceships and extracting knowledge and design information to build the crafts on Earth. Bushman also said the aliens have been working with American, Russian, and Chinese scientists to develop antigravity technology. In theory, antigravity devices could float above Earth using very little energy. (Most scientists believe antigravity is not possible due to the laws of physics.) Bushman, who states in the video that he does not believe anything if he has not seen real evidence, backed his claims with photographs said to be of aliens who died at Area 51.

When the video was posted to YouTube on October 24, several months after Bushman's death, it generated intense controversy. Ufologists used the video to justify their conspiracy theories, but skeptics called it a hoax. When Bushman's claims started to attract attention, a news outlet in Quebec pointed out that the aliens in the photographs strongly resembled plastic alien dolls available at Walmart. Bushman was called a charlatan seeking publicity and a prankster playing one last joke before his death. As research scientist Stuart J. Robbins explains:

> A deathbed confession can also be a way to solidify one's reputation by using the cultural belief . . . that people are 100% honest on their deathbed. . . . I find this whole deathbed confession thing unconvincing and, perhaps more importantly, not useful: We have no more information than we had before. We have no way to verify any of the information claimed. No way to test or duplicate it. At best, we have another person claiming this stuff is real.[32]

Abduction Explanations

Those who knew Bushman say that he truly believed in the existence of extraterrestrial beings. Psychologists who work with abductees say such beliefs are likely influenced more by media images than by reality. Researchers have found that filmed images of aliens, ghosts, vampires, and other paranormal creatures become deeply ingrained in the subconscious. The images can stick in a person's mind and play out in vivid dreams or daydreams.

Most people are aware that they are dreaming, even during the weirdest nightmares. But people with sleep disorders often have trouble telling where their dreams end and where reality begins. For example, those suffering from a disorder called sleep paralysis feel they are awake but they are unable to move. This condition, which can cause terror, is similar to what Copeland and others describe during alien encounters. Sleep paralysis also makes people feel as if they are floating. In this state, a person might hear loud buzzing and see flashing lights and aliens.

Psychologist Susan Clancy, who has worked with numerous alien abductees, has experienced sleep paralysis herself. She describes the feeling: "It was so powerful at the time. While I'm levitating in the air—that's what it felt like—and spinning like a rotisserie chicken. I had this feeling that something was a presence. And I was thinking, 'Oh, my God, it's real.' But then it was over and then I woke up."[33]

Unusual Ideas

Harvard University professor Richard J. McNally has worked with people he calls "sincere, nonpsychotic"[34] abductees. He discovered several traits common to those who believe they were abducted. Some were prone to a condition called false memory syndrome. During memory tests conducted on both abductees and nonabductees, McNally found that those with false memory syndrome regularly recalled hearing words and sentences that were never spoken. They also reported seeing images and items they were never shown. According to McNally, abductees were twice as likely as nonabductees to falsely remember things.

Abductees were also among a class of people with a mental trait called absorption, which made them prone to fantasy and easy to hypnotize. McNally believes this is an important factor since many abductees undergo hypnosis in an effort to clearly recall their hazy memories of abduction. While under hypnosis, abductees with absorption tend to use extremely vivid imagery in describing their experiences. Additionally, abductees are often asked leading questions by the hypnotist. For example, the hypnotist might wonder if the aliens were Greys. An abductee with absorption would then recall striking images of gray aliens like those seen in films.

Accounts of alien abductions are also more common among those who hold New Age beliefs. Members of the New Age movement, which developed during the 1970s, believe in concepts such as astrology, ghosts, alternative medicine, and fortune telling. People with these beliefs are prone to accept the existence of space aliens and other phenomena not easily explained by science. As McNally explains, "Anyone who entertains the possibility that aliens are routinely whisking earthlings up to spaceships, probing them medically, and [using them] for hybrid breeding tends to have unusual ideas."[35]

McNally found that the most common characteristic of abductees is a familiarity with what he called the cultural narrative of alien abduction:

Images of the typical alien are ubiquitous in American culture as are those of Santa Claus, and it is little wonder that abductees throughout the country report broadly similar kinds of alien encounters. . . . Alien contact narratives have closely tracked the appearance of the aliens and their spaceships as Hollywood has depicted them throughout the years. Bestselling books have provided further details of what it is like to be kidnapped by space aliens.[36]

A Deepened Spiritual Awareness

McNally points out that most abductees do not exhibit symptoms of illnesses such as depression or paranoia. In fact, some report that their abduction experiences were positive and gave them a new direction in life. For example, some abductees become environmentalists or peace activists who work to save the planet. Harvard psychology professor and abductee researcher John Mack explains: "People are confronted with the fate of the earth. They're shown scenes of the destruction of the earth, or apocalyptic images of portions of the earth being destroyed, and are told that the world can not go on in the way that we're living on it—treating the planet like it belongs to our species alone."[37]

Such experiences often shatter notions abductees have about the world and their place in it. Rather than seeing humanity as a driving force controlling Earth, abductees come to believe that there are mysterious forces more knowledgeable and powerful than people. This leads some contactees to find a deepened spiritual awareness within themselves. They believe they have gained mystical illumination, sometimes after receiving telepathic knowledge through intense eye-to-eye contact with aliens. This can leave abductees feeling as if they have telepathic powers or the ability to see into the future.

Love and Profound Intelligence

Seattle native Joy S. Gilbert is one contactee who believes her interactions with aliens led her down a path to spiritual enlightenment. She maintains a website describing her experiences with

According to some accounts, contact between humans and aliens begins with blue flashing lights and loud noises. In the midst of this chaos, the person is then transported into a large alien spacecraft.

space aliens over several decades. Gilbert says her first contact occurred in 1952 when she was three years old and was riding in the backseat of the family car. She remembers blue flashing lights and grinding noises as she was transported through the car window into a giant spacecraft she calls the Mother Ship. It was filled with aliens she calls Beings.

Gilbert was taken to a conference room with representatives from various star systems and regions of the universe. The meeting was overseen by a Being she calls the Chairman. The aliens at the table said they had met with leaders of every country on Earth hoping to convince them to live in peace. According to Gilbert, "The Chairman was pacing back and forth saying that Humans had proved over and over again that they could not develop compassion or love and their actions could not be tolerated. The Chairman spoke of destroying the Earth, obliterating the whole planet."[38] However, there were humans at the table who convinced the Chairman to give the people of Earth a chance to redeem themselves. Apparently permission was granted because Earth was not destroyed.

> "My experience with the Beings I have been involved with since my childhood . . . is one of soulful, interconnectedness, love, and profound intelligence."[39]
>
> —Joy S. Gilbert, alien contactee.

Gilbert had many more encounters with aliens throughout her life, most of which she felt were extremely positive. She says the experiences allowed her to read minds and see into the future. She describes herself as a translator and emissary between the alien world and the physical world. She believes that the Beings paired her with a mate, which allowed her to conceive children she calls star seeds, individuals from other star systems sent to Earth to boost the spiritual development of humanity. Gilbert sums up her feelings: "My experience with the Beings I have been involved with since my childhood . . . is one of soulful, interconnectedness, love, and profound intelligence. I experience . . . an utter sense of Universal Awareness, which causes me to experience a love for all life that transcends perception, thought, emotion, or physical attachments."[39]

Something Important Out There

Gilbert is among hundreds of contactees reporting similar feelings. Skeptics say this is a result of abductees reciting what is called a cultural script, which is a narrative of alien abductions repeated constantly over the years in the media. But Mack disputes the idea of a cultural script:

> People from all over the United States (and now from all over the world) have reported, with great concern for themselves and with much self-questioning, the same basic story of being visited and taken by aliens. . . . People didn't know each other, and they were shocked when they would hear that someone else had had the same kind of experience. I met some of these people very soon after that, and they seemed very sound of mind, very genuine and sincere to me.[40]

Although answers remain elusive, there is little doubt that people often search for a greater meaning to the universe. While many have feelings of insignificance while gazing up at the stars, believers feel that something important is occurring out there in space. They think aliens are paying attention to people and worrying about the misdeeds of the human race. This can provide feelings of comfort rather than stress when confronting earthly problems. Believers think that aliens devote considerable time and resources to raise humanity to a higher level of existence. Like ancient stories of angels and gods helping the sick and the needy, aliens are the modern-day version of caring spirits who provide solutions to every human need.

Chapter 3

The Search for Extraterrestrial Beings

"The human race is just a chemical scum on a moderate-sized planet, orbiting around a very average star in the outer suburb of one among a hundred billion galaxies."

—Stephen Hawking, theoretical physicist and cosmologist.
Quoted in David Deutsch, *The Fabric of Reality.* New York: Penguin, 1997, p. 177.

"Life like our own may be a very rare (if not singular), occurrence throughout all of time and space."

—Leanne Wendy Sharp, science journalist.
Leanne Wendy Sharp, "The Rare Earth Hypothesis," From Quarks to Quasars, May 4, 2014. www.fromquarkstoquasars.com.

Most tales told by alien abductees are easy to dismiss. Stories about extraterrestrials beaming people up into spaceships sound more like science fiction than science. But astronomers who search for life on other planets believe it is entirely possible that other beings exist somewhere in the vast universe. And in the twenty-first century, astronomers are seriously searching for those beings—or for other planets that might support life.

Astronomers estimate there are 70 sextillion stars in the universe. (That is the number 70 followed by 21 zeroes.) Scientists estimate at least 25 percent of those stars, around

17 sextillion, have planets orbiting them. These distant planets outside of Earth's solar system are called exoplanets. And if the figures are accurate, there are trillions of exoplanets in the limitless galaxies of the universe. Scientists estimate at least 10 percent of these planets might support life. Although most of this life is thought to be microscopic bacteria, some exoplanets could contain sentient, or conscious, life.

The Goldilocks Zone

Astronomers are discovering new Earth-like exoplanets every year. These planets exist in a small region of space, a habitable zone near a star that astronomers call the Goldilocks Zone. Because of Earth's location in relation to the Sun, Earth is also located in a Goldilocks Zone. The name is taken from the fairy tale "Goldilocks and the Three Bears" in which a girl named Goldilocks chooses porridge that is neither too hot nor too cold but just right. In the Goldilocks Zone, an exoplanet is neither too hot nor too cold; the orbit of the exoplanet around the parent star provides just the right conditions for surface water to exist. And according to most astrobiologists (scientists who study the possibility of life on other planets), water is a necessary ingredient for life.

In early 2015 astronomers announced the discovery of eight new exoplanets circling two stars. The first star, called Kepler-438b, is about 475 light-years from Earth; the second star, Kepler-442b, is 1,100 light-years away. Kepler-438b and Kepler-442b are both red dwarf stars. These types of stars are less than half the size of the Sun and generate about 10 percent of the Sun's luminosity, or light energy. Of the eight Kepler planets, two are in the Goldilocks Zone. David Kipping of the Harvard-Smithsonian Center for Astrophysics comments on the discovery: "We don't know for sure whether any of the planets in our sample are truly habitable. All we can say is that they're promising candidates."[41]

Kepler Discoveries

The Kepler stars are named after the seventeenth-century astronomer who believed aliens lived on Jupiter and its four moons. The planets were discovered by the *Kepler* space observatory, also named after the famed stargazer. The *Kepler* observatory was launched by NASA in 2009 to discover Earth-like exoplanets. The main instrument onboard *Kepler* is a photometer, an extremely sensitive instrument that monitors the brightness of over 145,000 stars. When exoplanets cross in front of their host stars, there is a periodic dimming that can be detected by NASA computers analyzing the data.

As of January 2015 *Kepler* had confirmed the existence of 1,013 exoplanets in 440 star systems. An additional 3,200 possible exoplanets remain unconfirmed. Based on *Kepler* data, scientists estimate there are as many as 40 billion Earth-sized planets orbiting Goldilocks Zones in the Milky Way galaxy alone.

An illustration depicts the **Kepler** *space telescope observing planets transiting a distant star.* **Kepler** *is searching for exoplanets that may have conditions suitable to support life.*

The Rare Earth Hypothesis

Although NASA astronomers speculate about extraterrestrials living on Goldilocks exoplanets, there are those who doubt life can exist in distant solar systems and galaxies. The exoplanet skeptics point to a theory called the rare earth hypothesis devised by Peter Ward, a geologist and paleontologist, and Donald E. Brownlee, an astronomer and astrobiologist.

According to the rare earth hypothesis, life developed on Earth due to extremely specific circumstances. These conditions, which include the nature of Earth, the Sun, and other planets in the solar system, are rare or nonexistent elsewhere in the universe. If, however, life were to develop on a distant exoplanet, the parent star would need to be the size and luminosity of the Sun. The red dwarfs that make up the Kepler stars are too small and dull to fit these requirements. Additionally, a populated exoplanet would have to have the right type of atmosphere and temperature so water would not boil or freeze. The exoplanet would also need a stable orbit so it would not veer too close, or too far, from its star.

Even if an exoplanet and star fit these requirements, other conditions would have to be met to sustain life. For example, Earth's axis is tilted at an angle of 23.5°. Because of this tilt, most of Earth has four moderate seasons. For life to develop on an exoplanet, its axis would need to tilt at a similar angle. Additionally, the exoplanet would need a rotational speed similar to Earth's to provide periods of day and night necessary for plant and animal evolution.

Comets and Radiation

Another element of the rare earth hypothesis concerns the size and location of Jupiter in the solar system. Astronomers believe that life evolved on Earth, in part, because of Jupiter. The huge planet protects Earth from collisions with long-period comets— that is, meteors that take more than two hundred years to orbit the Sun. Science journalist Deborah Byrd explains: "[Long-period comets] enter the solar system from its outer reaches. Jupiter's gravity is thought to sling most of these fast-moving ice balls out of the solar system before they can get close to Earth. . . . Without Jupiter nearby, long-period comets would collide with our planet much more frequently."[42]

Although small meteorites hit Earth every day, if a big comet crashed into the planet it would cause major devastation. If a comet landed in the ocean, the resulting tsunamis would wipe out coastal cities. A comet hitting a landmass would start massive wildfires so intense that the smoke and ash would blot out the sun for months. Plants would die, and animals would have nothing to eat. Scientists believe that the last time a large comet collided with Earth was 65 million years ago, and the devastation wiped out the dinosaurs.

Another aspect that allowed life to evolve on Earth has to do with the distance of the Sun from other stars, what is called a favorable galactic zone. If there were other nearby stars, giving Earth two or more suns, life would not have evolved as it has. Other factors in the favorable galactic zone include the absence of collapsing or exploding stars and the lack of black holes, which would cause a devastating gravitational pull.

The Mediocrity Principle

Not surprisingly, there is an alternative argument to the rare earth hypothesis called the mediocrity principle. The theory, popularized by Carl Sagan, is backed by those who believe alien life exists in other parts of the universe. (The term *mediocre*, while often used to denote something that is of poor quality, also means "commonplace.") The mediocrity principle states that there is nothing special or rare about Earth's particular position in relation to the Sun or other planets. According to the mediocrity principle, the conditions that allowed human life to develop are commonplace among the sextillions of stars and planets. As astronomer Andrew Howard states, Earth-like planets "are like grains of sand sprinkled on a beach—they are everywhere."[43]

> "[Earth-like planets] are like grains of sand sprinkled on a beach—they are everywhere."[43]
>
> —Andrew Howard, astronomer.

The likelihood of there being other inhabited planets does not mean, however, that the beings that populate those Earth-like

"Listen Before We Shout"

In February 2015 twenty-eight prominent scientists and space experts circulated a petition calling for an end to programs known as METI (Messaging to Extraterrestrial Intelligence), which are meant to contact extraterrestrial intelligence (ETI). The petition is excerpted below:

> ETI's reaction to a message from Earth cannot presently be known. We know nothing of ETI's intentions and capabilities, and it is impossible to predict whether ETI will be benign or hostile.

> Because we have just recently (in cosmic terms) attained an interstellar communications capability, it is likely that other communicative civilizations we encounter will be millions of years more advanced than us.

> The Search for Extraterrestrial Intelligence (SETI), the scientific effort to determine whether or not other advanced life exists in the universe, is still in its infancy. . . . As a newly emerging technological species, it is prudent to listen before we shout.

> Although a nearby advanced ETI may have already picked up earth's omni-directional radio leakage, e.g., early television transmissions, or the presence of industrial wastes in the atmosphere of the earth, such detections are far more difficult than detecting a focused radio or optical signal sent from a large telescope.

> It is not necessary to actually transmit powerful electromagnetic signals in order to study interstellar communication from the perspective of the transmitter, or to develop transmission techniques that might one day be used to respond to a message received from an ETI.

Armando Azua-Bustos et al., "Regarding Messaging to Extraterrestrial Intelligence (METI) / Active Searches for Extraterrestrial Intelligence (Active SETI)," SETI@Home, 2015. https://setiathome.berkeley.edu.

planets will be exactly like human beings. They might be less intellectually developed than twenty-first-century humans. Or they might be much more evolved. If an alien civilization was even one thousand years ahead of modern Earth society, it could have technology so advanced that humans could not possibly comprehend it. If an alien race were 1 million years more developed, it might be as incomprehensible as modern civilization is to a monkey. As renowned science fiction writer Arthur C. Clarke put it, "Any sufficiently advanced technology is indistinguishable from magic."[44]

> "Any sufficiently advanced technology is indistinguishable from magic."[44]
>
> —*Arthur C. Clarke, science fiction author.*

With the understanding that intelligence likely evolves at different rates on alien planets, a Russian scientist named Nikolai Kardashev devised the Kardashev Scale. This scale is used to measure a society's level of technological advancement. The Kardashev Scale has three designated levels: Type I, Type II, and Type III. These are based on the amount of usable energy a civilization has at its disposal and its relationship to nearby stars and planets.

Earth is a Type I planet because it is very close to utilizing all of its available energy sources. These include fossil fuels, nuclear power, and renewable energy sources such as hydroelectric, solar, and wind. A Type II society can harness all the energy provided by its host star. This ability goes far beyond building solar panels. A Type II society might use advanced technology to perform what is called star lifting. In this process, a large portion of a star would be removed and captured for use in a controlled manner to provide endless energy. A Type II society might also have the ability to move entire planets. These could be put in place to enclose a star and harvest all of its solar energy.

A Type III society would have more abilities than a Type II civilization. It might be able to tap the energy released by black holes that are thought to exist at the center of galaxies. Type III civilizations might also be able to harvest electromagnetic radiation from gamma rays or other sources of energy currently unknown to scientists.

The Search for Extraterrestrial Intelligence

Programs aimed at finding Type I, II, and III alien societies are known by two acronyms: SETI (Search for Extraterrestrial Intelligence) and METI (Messaging to Extraterrestrial Intelligence). Physicists, astrobiologists, and astronomers involved with SETI scan the skies seeking radio frequency signals produced by civilizations on distant planets. Those involved with METI send specially prepared signals into space hoping they will be received and decoded by an alien race that might provide a reply.

One of the first mentions of SETI occurred in 1959 when physicists Giuseppe Cocconi and Philip Morrison wrote in *Nature* magazine, "[Near] some star rather like the Sun there are civilizations with scientific interests and with technical possibilities much greater than those now available to us. . . . We shall assume that long ago they established a channel of communication that would one day become known to us, and that they look forward patiently to the answering signals from [us]."[45]

Project Ozma

In 1960 the *Nature* article inspired radio astronomer Frank Drake to begin the search for alien communications using the National Radio Astronomy Observatory in Green Bank, West Virginia. Drake called his exploration Project Ozma after the fictional Princess Ozma in the Land of Oz books by L. Frank Baum. Drake picked the name because Oz was described as a place "very far away, difficult to reach, and populated by strange and exotic beings."[46]

Drake initiated the search by pointing the 85-foot (26 m) parabolic dish of the radio telescope at two Sun-like stars, Epsilon Eridani and Tau Ceti, located around eleven light-years from Earth. Drake was hoping the telescope would pick up radio waves alien civilizations were using to communicate. Radio waves, which include microwaves, visible light, and X-rays, are produced by electromagnetic radiation. The waves are emitted throughout the universe by natural forces and move through space at the speed of light. On Earth, electromagnetic waves are used for broadcasting signals to radios, televisions, cell phones, satellites, and radar instruments. These long-lasting waves, called artifact signals, could also be produced by extraterrestrial civilizations.

A radio telescope focuses incoming radio waves onto a small antenna referred to as the feed. Information from the feed can be viewed on a monitor by radio astronomers and analyzed by computers. When searching for intelligent life, the telescopes act as extremely sensitive receivers that collect faint electromagnetic waves that might be produced on other planets.

By 1964 Drake determined that his attempt to receive extraterrestrial signals was a failure. Rather than quit, he devised a formula called the Drake equation to keep interest in SETI alive. The Drake equation, based on the mediocrity principle, is a complex mathematical formula that takes into account the estimated num-

Frank Drake began the search for alien communications with the help of the National Radio Astronomy Observatory, a radio telescope (pictured) near Green Bank, West Virginia. Though he never achieved his goal, Drake's work continues to inspire the search for extraterrestrial life.

ber of planets orbiting in Goldilocks Zones around stars. In 1965, when Drake published the equation, he estimated there were ten thousand planets in the Milky Way that could harbor intelligent life capable of communicating with Earth.

Astronomers inspired by the Drake equation continued to hunt for alien radio signals for decades. However, in 2010, at the age of eighty, Drake conceded that not a single alien message had ever been received. Explanations for the failure of SETI were numerous: perhaps aliens do not exist, they are too far away, they are not advanced enough to produce radio signals, or they communicate using some other method.

Despite the SETI failures to connect with aliens, Drake stood by his equation. And in recent years the equation has been confirmed and updated with new information based on observations by the *Kepler* space observatory and other powerful telescopes. In 2015 the Drake equation estimated the number of Earth-like planets in the Milky Way to be around 40 billion. According to Drake, the mediocrity principle is still valid:

> "The observations have all supported the idea that there is a lot of life in the universe. . . . That includes the evolution of an intelligent technology-using creature."[47]
>
> —*Frank Drake, radio astronomer.*

> The observations have all supported the idea that there is a lot of life in the universe. What they show is that what happened in the Solar System was not unusual. It did not require any special circumstances, or any freak situations, and therefore what happened here should have happened in many places, and that includes the evolution of an intelligent technology-using creature.[47]

"Where Is Everybody?"

Whatever the number of Earth-like planets, skeptics continue to believe SETI projects are a waste of time and money. Many of these doubters subscribe to what is called the Fermi Paradox.

The theory devised by physicist Enrico Fermi in 1950 points out a contradiction, or paradox: if there are billions of inhabitable planets capable of supporting life, where are the advanced civilizations? In more modern terms, if the galaxy is teeming with aliens, why doesn't the universe look like a *Star Wars* movie? The SETI Institute, which utilizes an array of radio telescopes to detect alien signals, explains the Fermi Paradox on its website:

> Fermi realized that any civilization with a modest amount of rocket technology and an immodest amount of imperial incentive [the desire to conquer other planets] could rapidly colonize the entire Galaxy. Within ten million years, every star system could be brought under the wing of empire. Ten million years may sound long, but in fact it's quite short compared with the age of the Galaxy, which is roughly ten thousand million years. Colonization of the Milky Way should be a quick exercise. . . . This prompted Fermi to ask what was (to him) an obvious question: "where is everybody?"[48]

As Fermi noted, the galaxy does not appear to teem with life, and there have been no credible reports of visitations or communications with alien races. However, astronomers who spend their time searching for extraterrestrial intelligence have devised answers to the Fermi Paradox.

Some argue that space travel simply takes too much energy; a spacecraft traveling at 10 percent, or even 1 percent, the speed of light would consume more energy than it could carry. Others answer the paradox by saying the galaxy might be colonized, but humanity simply does not notice. Perhaps aliens are invisible or their bodies are similar to light waves or radio waves. In this manner of thinking, aliens might be observing humanity, but people cannot observe them.

Revealing Waves of Sound

If advanced alien societies were monitoring the universe for radio waves, they might know quite a bit about human activities.

The Benefits of Alien Contact

In 1960 radio astronomer Frank Drake was the first to use a telescope to search the galaxy for radio waves produced by advanced alien societies. Although Drake's search for extraterrestrial intelligence failed, he continued to believe technologically advanced creatures inhabit the universe. In 2010 Drake described the influence of such aliens if they were to be discovered, and the difficulties involved in discovering them:

> It will have a tremendous impact because almost any civilization we find will be much older than our own. They will have much more experience. Much more knowledge, technical and scientific. And that will benefit us greatly. And we will learn ways to have a higher quality of life on earth which would otherwise take us perhaps hundreds of years of expensive research to learn, to identify ourselves. . . . [But] probably only one in ten million stars has a detectable signal. We haven't nearly searched that many stars. . . . Also the signals may be transient, they may not be "on" all the time, so we need to search tens of millions of stars for long periods of time on a wide band of frequencies, before we'll have a good chance of succeeding.

Quoted in Wilson da Silva, "Finding Aliens 'Only a Matter of Time,'" *Cosmos*, February 2010. www.wilsondasilva.com.

Civilization has been beaming nonstop broadcast signals into space at the speed of light since the beginning of commercial radio broadcasting during the early 1920s. If radio astronomers existed on the exoplanet Gliese-526, 17.6 light-years from Earth, they would have picked up those first radio shows around 1938.

The electronic chatter increased greatly after the advent of television during the 1950s. Since that time, broadcast waves

Broadcast waves from television shows ranging from the Beverly Hillbillies *to* The Walking Dead *(pictured) have been beaming through space. Advanced alien societies that might encounter these signals are likely to be confused, amused, or horrified by the civilization that created these shows.*

of every television program—from *The Beverly Hillbillies* of the 1960s to the latest twenty-first-century zombie show—have been hurtling through space. And these waves might confuse, amuse, or horrify technically proficient aliens. Astrophysicist and science communicator Neil deGrasse Tyson comments on the possibility: "For all we know, the aliens have already [heard all] this and . . . concluded that there was no intelligent life on Earth."[49]

Cosmic Calls

While Tyson jokes, METI scientists are serious about using powerful radio telescopes to initiate communications with alien civilizations. The first attempt occurred in 1999, when Canadian astrophysicists Yvan Dutil and Stephane Dumas sent a message named the Cosmic Call. It contained digital code that described basic concepts of math, physics, chemistry, and biology. The Cosmic Call was sent into space from a Russian radio telescope called the Evpatoria Planetary Radar (EPR) in Crimea, Ukraine.

In 2001 a second call, known as the Teen Age Message (TAM) was sent from the EPR. The project, organized by Russian radio astronomer Alexander L. Zaitsev, was so named because it contained ideas from student scientists in Russia. The TAM contained music, including Russian folk songs, the 1966 Beach Boys hit "Good Vibrations," and the finale of Beethoven's Ninth Symphony. It also contained digital photos and text information with greetings from the teens to aliens, written both in Russian and English. The TAM lasted two hours and twelve minutes and was transmitted several times between August 29 and September 4, 2001. In 2003 Zaitsev sent the Cosmic Call 2 to five Sun-like stars. He estimated the message would reach the star Hip-4872 in the Cassiopeia constellation in 2036 and the star HD-95128 in the Cygnus constellation in 2049.

In 2008 NASA launched its own METI message, beaming the Beatles' song "Across the Universe" toward the North Star. That same year an Arctic transmitter run by a consortium of European and Asian nations was used by the Frito-Lay corporation to broadcast a Doritos commercial to a star forty-two light-years away.

METI Critics

The METI broadcasts have been criticized by those who fear the signals might attract a hostile race of aliens to Earth. In 2010 renowned British physicist Stephen Hawking made headlines with this warning:

> We only have to look at ourselves to see how intelligent life might develop into something we wouldn't want to meet. I imagine they might exist in massive ships, having used up

all the resources from their home planet. Such advanced aliens would perhaps become nomads, looking to conquer and colonize whatever planets they can reach. . . . I think the outcome would be much as when Christopher Columbus first landed in America, which didn't turn out very well for the Native Americans.[50]

Hawking's words might sound like something from a science fiction film, but his views are backed by other prominent METI critics. They include Geoff Marcy, discoverer of seventy exoplanets; Elon Musk, whose company SpaceX builds rockets that service the International Space Station; and David Brin, a scientist and award-winning science fiction author.

In 2015 Brin, Marcy, Musk, and twenty-five other space experts signed an anti-METI petition. The petition stated that it is impossible to predict whether extraterrestrial life will be benign or hostile and warned against sending out extraterrestrial messages: "METI programs carry unknown and potentially enormous implications and consequences. We feel the decision whether or not to transmit must be based upon a worldwide consensus, and not a decision based upon the wishes of a few individuals with access to powerful communications equipment."[51]

Not everyone agrees with such sentiments. Douglas A. Vakoch is the director of interstellar message composition at the SETI Institute in Mountain View, California. Vakoch believes that messaging extraterrestrials is the only way to find out if humanity is alone in the universe. He also thinks aliens might have advanced technology that could solve problems on Earth. Vakoch, who one day hopes to beam space messages with powerful lasers, says there is no danger of an alien invasion. According to Vakoch, the messages are an "attempt to join the galactic club."[52] Brin disagrees with Vakoch's sunny state-

"We only have to look at ourselves to see how intelligent life might develop into something we wouldn't want to meet. . . . Such advanced aliens would perhaps become nomads, looking to conquer and colonize whatever planets they can reach."[50]

—Stephen Hawking, theoretical physicist.

ments: "I can't bring myself to wager my grandchildren's destiny on unreliable assumptions"[53] about kindly aliens.

Whatever the fears of an alien invasion, humanity continues to reveal itself—and not only through radio and television broadcasts. Electromagnetic waves from radar installations, telecommunications satellites, and other sources make Earth one of the noisiest places in the universe. So while astronomers search the skies for exoplanets and radio waves, a federation of advanced civilizations might be listening to activities on Earth with wonder or concern. And they might be planning a journey to Earth at any moment.

Chapter 4

Are There Other Explanations for Space Aliens?

"If these events surrounding [space aliens crashing at] Roswell in the summer of 1947 actually took place . . . it is an understatement to say that such a revelation would fundamentally transform humanity as we know it."

—Kal K. Korff, computer pioneer and ufologist.

Kal K. Korff, "What Really Happened at Roswell," *Skeptical Inquirer*, July/August 1997. www.csicop.org.

"The media capitalized on 'the Roswell incident,' and conspiracy theorists, persons with confabulated memories, outright hoaxers, and others climbed aboard the bandwagon."

—Joe Nickell and James McGaha, members of the Committee for Skeptical Inquiry.

Joe Nickell and James McGaha, "The Roswellian Syndrome: How Some UFO Myths Develop," *Skeptical Inquirer*, May/June 2012. www.csicop.org.

During the fourteenth century, an English friar named William of Ockham pondered complex questions about science, philosophy, and God. While doing so he came up with a problem-solving principle called Ockham's razor. According to Ockham's razor, when a person is searching for an explanation for an unexplainable event, the simplest answer is most often the correct one.

Ockham's razor is sometimes invoked in contemporary debates about the existence of aliens. Whereas believers provide complex theories about aliens traveling billions of miles to Earth in technically advanced spaceships, doubters cite Ockham's razor. They say there are simple explanations behind UFO sightings. For example, many UFOs have been attributed to natural weather phenomena known as lightning sprites. These massive electrical discharges occur high above pancake-shaped thunderstorm clouds and, at times, can look like a fleet of UFOs. Sprites—which might have a red, pink, or blue hue—are a naturally occurring, although rare, phenomenon that was not discovered until 1989.

A red sprite, rarely ever photographed, is captured on film by a joint project of NASA and the University of Alaska, Fairbanks. Sprites, which last for only a few milliseconds and are barely visible to the naked eye, might explain some UFO sightings.

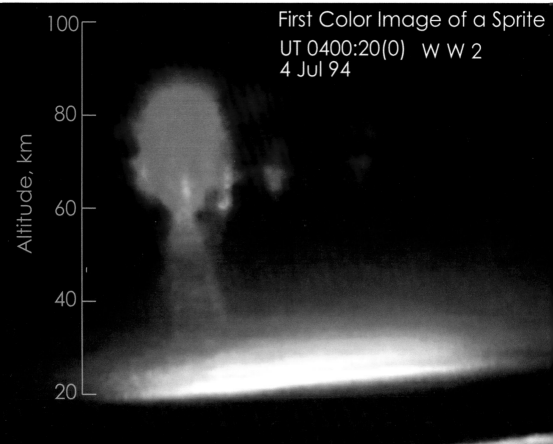

First Color Image of a Sprite
UT 0400:20(0) W W 2
4 Jul 94

Missiles and the U-2

Many UFO sightings over the years have been attributed to top secret government tests of weapons and aircraft. During the Cold War, which lasted from the late 1940s into the 1990s, the United States and the Soviet Union were engaged in an arms race. Each side built thousands of intercontinental ballistic missiles to carry powerful nuclear weapons. When the US missiles were tested in Nevada and New Mexico during this period, they sometimes produced green fireballs—a sight that generated numerous UFO reports.

During the Cold War, the United States also built several generations of radar-evading warplanes and spy planes. These ventures were highly classified, and their existence was only known to those working on the projects. One top secret spy plane, the U-2, had the capability of photographing Soviet military installations. During the mid-1950s, when the CIA and Air Force tested the U-2 at Area 51 in Nevada, the flights always corresponded with an increase in UFO reports from commercial airline pilots. This is notable because pilots are often said to be the most sober, reliable sources for UFO reports.

With its advanced design, it is not surprising the U-2 was mistaken for a UFO. The U-2 had wings that were twice as long as its fuselage. When the wings reflected bright sunlight, the plane looked like a fiery cross streaking across the sky. The U-2 also flew at the extremely high altitude of 70,000 feet (21,336 m). During this era most people did not believe manned flight was possible above 60,000 feet (18,288 m). Commercial airliners of the time flew at altitudes between 10,000 and 20,000 feet (3,048 and 6,096 m). It is little wonder pilots thought they were seeing a glimmering UFO flying 50,000 feet (15,240 m) above their aircraft.

Skeptics have long believed that the high-altitude U-2 flights were responsible for around half of all UFO reports. The CIA confirmed this belief after the agency moved into the world of social media and opened a Twitter account in June 2014. While sharing nonclassified information about its activities with 760,000 followers, the CIA occasionally makes light of UFO controversies. In December 2014 the agency tweeted, "Reports of unusual activity in the skies in the '50s? It was us."[54]

A Strange Sighting in Roswell

Secretive Air Force tests were also at the center of the so-called Roswell incident, a purported UFO crash in the vicinity of Roswell, New Mexico. The Roswell incident began on July 2, 1947, during an intense rainstorm. Residents in the sparsely populated area heard a loud crashing sound near Foster Ranch approximately 30 miles (48 km) north of Roswell. On July 4, ranch foreman William "Mac" Brazel and his seventy-year-old neighbor, William "Dee" Proctor, set out to look for evidence of an airplane crash among the brush and rocks. The men did not find an aircraft. Instead, what they found were large and small pieces of extremely lightweight, shiny material unlike anything they had ever seen before. Some pieces had incomprehensible letters or symbols that reminded Brazel of ancient Native American petroglyphs found in the region.

> "Reports of unusual activity in the skies in the '50s? It was us."[54]
>
> —*The CIA, tweeting in 2014.*

Brazel later reported that the debris was scattered over an area of burned ground about 0.75 miles (1.2 km) long and 200 feet (61 m) wide. Later in the day, Brazel showed pieces of the strange objects to his children. In 1980 Brazel's son described the debris:

> [It was] something on the order of tinfoil, except that [it] wouldn't tear. . . . You could wrinkle it and lay it back down and it immediately resumed its original shape . . . quite pliable, but you couldn't crease or bend it like ordinary metal. Almost like a plastic, but definitely metallic. Dad once said that the Army had told him it was not anything made by us.[55]

In this era, before television, Brazel was unaware of the UFO craze sweeping the country. However, his neighbors had heard that a national magazine was offering $3,000 to anyone who could provide physical evidence of a UFO. It is unknown whether Brazel was motivated by this rumor, but some skeptics believe his actions in the following days were motivated by hopes of monetary gain.

A Flying Saucer Is Captured

After the discovery on Foster Ranch, the Roswell story took on a life of its own. Brazel showed pieces of the debris to Chaves County sheriff George A. Wilcox. Wilcox contacted the nearby Roswell Army Air Field (RAAF), home to the 509th Bomb Wing. In the meantime, Walter Whitmore, owner of local radio station KGFL, had heard about the incident and did an on-air interview with Brazel.

Hours after the interview was broadcast on KGFL, Lieutenant Walter Haut from the RAAF arrived at the station. Haut carried a press release written by the base commander stating that the US Army Air Corps (later renamed the Air Force) had retrieved a flying disc from Foster Ranch. A reporter read the press release on the air and sent it out on the Associated Press (AP) newswire. The AP forwarded the statement to newspapers and radio stations throughout the world. Within hours, stories about the flying saucer discovery appeared in major newspapers, including the *Chicago Daily News*, *Los Angeles Herald Express*, and the *San Francisco Examiner*. The evening edition of the *Roswell Daily Record* printed a front-page story announcing, "RAAF Captures Flying Saucer on Ranch in Roswell Region."[56]

After the Roswell incident made national headlines, Brigadier General Roger Ramey, head of the Eighth Army Air Corps, attempted to retract the story. At a hastily arranged press conference, Ramey told reporters that the alleged flying saucer was nothing more than a weather balloon. Those who lived around Roswell doubted Ramey's story. The Air Corps had closed off a huge area around Foster Ranch, an action that suggested something more unusual than a weather balloon.

The Three-Crash Theory

In what was called a top secret recovery mission, dozens of Air Corps crash specialists began combing through the sand at the crash site. While workers loaded debris onto flatbed trucks, numerous military police (MPs) kept onlookers and reporters away from the site. Local residents reported that tanks were used to close

UFOs and the CIA

In the early 1950s the CIA, headed by General Walter Bedell Smith, was in charge of monitoring Soviet activities with spies, radar, spy planes, and other equipment. General Smith believed UFOs and aliens were nothing more than paranoid fantasies dreamed up by a nervous public fearing nuclear war. But Smith had a problem: he worried that Soviet leader Joseph Stalin might order a fake UFO attack to panic the American public. Smith was concerned about the US government's ability to maintain control in such a situation. He also feared that important government communications equipment would be overloaded by calls from terrified citizens.

In 1952 Smith put together the Psychological Strategy Board to address concerns involving UFOs and aliens. According to top secret CIA documents released to the public in 1993, the board proposed a major alien-debunking campaign in the mass media. The agency wanted newspapers and news programs to mock people who believed in aliens. The CIA also considered enlisting ad executives, business leaders, and even Walt Disney in the campaign. However, the media had little interest in debunking the belief in UFOs. Stories about UFOs sold a large number of newspapers and magazines, and alien invasions were regular subjects of films and television shows.

roads, and barricades were manned by MPs holding machine guns. A diary kept by one resident, Ted Anderson, stated, "The Military is . . . making a lot of noise about what could happen to traitors and that you could get shot for talking about military secrets."[57]

The urgent and secretive way the military handled the investigation made Foster Ranch ground zero for countless conspiracy theories in later years. The central questions revolved around the 15-mile (24 km) perimeter the Air Corps had set up around the original crash site. Ufologists believe that the large area contained three separate crash sites.

The three-crash theory was put forth in 1980 in *The Roswell Incident* by Charles Berlitz and William Moore. The book was the first written about the incident and was based on ninety interviews conducted in the area by nuclear physicist and ufologist Stanton T. Friedman. According to *The Roswell Incident*, an alien space-

Brigadier General Roger Ramey (left) identifies metallic fragments found in 1947 near Roswell, New Mexico, as pieces of a weather balloon. Many doubters think Ramey's comments were part of a cover-up of alien visitation.

craft was flying over the New Mexico desert monitoring nuclear weapons tests when it crashed after being hit by lightning. (The book did not explain how a spacecraft that had traveled billions of miles through space was downed by lightning.)

The Roswell Incident goes on to describe three separate crash sites. The first, according to the book, contained the debris originally discovered by Brazel. A second site, a few miles away, is where the main body of an alien spacecraft supposedly crashed. A third site, several miles farther, contained what the book describes as a crashed UFO "escape capsule." Inside the capsule, the book states, were four space aliens, one alive, one dying, and two dead. The aliens were said to have yellow skin, large heads, no hair, and small bodies. According to Dan Dwyer, a Roswell fireman who said he inspected the site before the military arrived, the surviving alien "was about the size of a 10 year old child, and it didn't have any hair. . . . It seemed scared, lost, and afraid."[58]

> "[The alien] was about the size of a 10 year old child, and it didn't have any hair. . . . It seemed scared, lost, and afraid."[58]
>
> —Dan Dwyer, Roswell fireman.

A Sketch of the Bodies

After *The Roswell Incident* was published, the event became the focus of numerous books and television shows. The story of child-like aliens was revived in the 1991 book *UFO Crash at Roswell* by Kevin D. Randle and Donald R. Schmitt. The *UFO Crash at Roswell* contains a story told by Glenn Dennis, a mortician at Ballard's Funeral Home in Roswell in 1947. Dennis said that after the crash he was contacted by a mortuary officer at the RAAF who inquired about obtaining three child-sized coffins that would be airtight when sealed. The officer also asked Dennis about preparing a body that had been exposed to the elements or burned in a crash. Additionally, Dennis was asked about techniques used to preserve a body, blood, and organs that did not require embalming. Dennis suggested packing the material in dry ice and offered to help the officer with his task. His offer was refused.

Dennis was curious, so he drove out to the airfield. When he entered the base infirmary, Dennis says he was grabbed under each arm by two MPs who roughly escorted him from the building. The MPs then followed his car back to town. Later that night he said he received a threatening phone call from the base officer warning him to stop looking into the matter. Ignoring the threat, Dennis drove back to the RAAF the next day, where he spoke to a friend, Naomi Maria Selff, who was a nurse on the base.

Selff told Dennis that she had entered an examination room the night before where doctors were conducting autopsies on three dead aliens who were burned and mangled. She said the room smelled so bad that it made her gag. Selff then showed Dennis drawings she had made of the aliens. Dennis later described them:

> She drew me a sketch of the bodies, including an arm with a hand that had only four fingers; the doctors noted that on the end of the fingers were little pads resembling suction cups. She said the head was disproportionately large for the body; the eyes were deeply set; the skulls were flexible; the nose was concave . . . the mouth was a fine slit, and the doctors said there was heavy cartilage instead of teeth. The ears were only small orifices with flaps. They had no hair, and the skin was black—perhaps due to exposure in the sun. . . . They were three-and-a-half to four feet tall.[59]

Skeptics had many reasons to doubt Dennis's story: he never saw the aliens, he said he inexplicably threw out the alien drawings made by the nurse, and journalists checking military records could find no mention of Selff. Adding to suspicion of a hoax, Dennis waited more than four decades to come forth with the story. When he finally did go public, his story coincided with numerous books being written and resurging interest in what might have taken place at Roswell.

Bizarre Experiments

Aliens at Roswell made the news once again in 2011 after investigative journalist Annie Jacobsen wrote *Area 51: An Uncensored History of America's Top-Secret Military Base.* Jacobsen's sources for the book were members of a once-secret club called the Roadrunners, made up of retired Area 51 employees who met on a regular basis.

Ufologists had long suspected that the debris from the Roswell crash was studied and stored at Area 51. According to one aerospace engineer interviewed by Jacobsen, this suspicion was true. And the unidentified object from Roswell was a real flying disc; but it was not of alien origins. The craft, Jacobsen writes, was made in the Soviet Union and sent flying across New Mexico on the orders of Soviet leader Joseph Stalin. Engineers at Area 51 who studied the craft did not understand the technology that made the saucer fly or hover. General Walter Bedell Smith, head of the CIA, believed he knew why the flying disc was sent to the United States: Stalin was attempting to create mass hysteria among the public by creating a phony alien attack.

> "The head was disproportionately large for the body; the eyes were deeply set; the skulls were flexible; the nose was concave . . . the mouth was a fine slit."[59]
>
> —*Glenn Dennis, Roswell mortician.*

Jacobsen's book outlines an even more bizarre explanation for the supposed alien bodies seen at the crash site. She contends that the fliers were teenagers deliberately deformed to look like aliens. This was supposedly done through ghastly medical procedures performed by the German doctor Josef Mengele. During World War II, Mengele conducted gruesome medical experiments on children and other prisoners at the Auschwitz concentration camp.

In 1945, near the end of the war, Mengele fled Auschwitz to avoid capture by Soviet forces. Historians say he eventually immigrated to Argentina in South America. However, Jacobsen contends he spent several years in the Soviet Union. She says Stalin asked Mengele to physically transform a small group of Soviet orphans into alien-like beings. Supposedly, Stalin hoped the children would be mistaken for visitors from Mars when they emerged from the craft. Jacobsen contends that Stalin's UFO hoax was never revealed to the American public because President Harry Truman did not want it known that Soviet aircraft—or, in this case, spaceships, had easily reached US soil.

Failing the "Smell Test"

Like many tales of Roswell aliens, skeptics have analyzed and dismissed Jacobsen's claims. The main source of the story was an unnamed retired engineer who worked for a government contractor. Jacobsen does not explain why an aerospace engineer would be examining alien bodies or how he would know they were surgically altered. The engineer also claims the bodies were genetically altered, but the structure of the genetic material DNA was not discovered until 1953. As author and Skeptics Society member Donald Prothero explains,

> If the "teenagers" were genetically engineered by the Soviets using Mengele, they would have to have grown up remarkably fast in the two years from 1945 when Soviets occupied Berlin until 1947, when the Roswell incident took place. In addition, this supposedly all took place over 64 years ago, and this alleged "engineer" would have to be at least in his 30s to have the training and experience to hold such a job. If you do the math, he's in his 90s or older. Doesn't that strike anyone as suspicious? Doesn't that fail the "smell test" of credibility for most people?[60]

When asked about the discrepancies in her book by interviewer Terry Gross on the National Public Radio show *Fresh Air*, Jacobsen simply said she did not think the engineer was lying. Whatever the case, *Area 51* received a great deal of publicity when it was published and provided a strange, if unlikely, explanation for the incident.

Project Mogul

Jacobsen's book ignores two Air Force reports released during the 1990s. These reports conclude that the craft that crashed near Roswell was part of a top secret US spy program called Project Mogul. At the time, the Soviet Union was working to develop its first hydrogen bomb (H-bomb). Project Mogul utilized high-altitude balloons loaded with sensitive acoustic sensors meant

There's an App for That

People wishing to prove the existence of aliens and UFOs regularly publish photos and videos of extraterrestrials on websites. But such alleged proof is often a product of pranksters and charlatans. Over the years alien and UFO photos were often staged with plastic dolls, alien masks, and flying pie plates. But in the high-tech age, there is an app for that; iPhone and Android photo apps allow users to create their own "proof" of aliens and UFOs.

Apps like UFO Camera Gold and UFO Photo Bomb allow users to select from a variety of UFO types and place them anywhere in their photographs. The size, shape, and transparency of the UFOs can be easily adjusted. The UFO Photo Art app even allows users to add spaceships to their smartphone videos. Those who wish to actually look like space aliens can use Alien Booth. This app transforms selfies and pictures of friends, family, and even pets into strange-looking aliens. While these apps can be fun, the fake photos are sometimes shown on television or printed in newspaper stories. The fakes are not high quality, but according to ufologist Frank Warren, "for most seasoned Ufologists the hoaxed photos are blatantly obvious; unfortunately, that minority won't stop the MSM [mainstream media] from paying heed to the latest hokum produced."

Quoted in Robert Sheaffer, "UFO Hoaxes? There's an App for That!," *Skeptical Inquirer*, November/December 2013. www.csicop.org.

to detect sound waves generated by Soviet nuclear explosions. The program operated out of the Alamogordo Army Airfield, now Holloman Air Force Base (AFB), located about 135 miles (217 km) northwest of Roswell.

The balloons used in Project Mogul were made of polyethylene plastic, used today in everything from plastic bags and food containers to cars and computers. However, plastic was not widely used in consumer goods until the 1950s. It is doubtful that rural residents in 1947 New Mexico were aware that plastic existed or that it was used to make secret spy craft. First Lieutenant James McAndrew, who wrote a 1997 Air Force report on Roswell, explains:

> During the late 1940's and 1950's, a characteristic associated with the large, newly invented, polyethylene balloons, was that they were often misidentified as flying saucers. During this period, polyethylene balloons launched at Holloman AFB generated flying saucer reports on nearly every flight. Also, the balloons, flown at altitudes of approximately 100,000 feet [30,480 m], were illuminated . . . just after sunset and just before sunrise . . . [appearing] as large bright objects against a dark sky.[61]

The balloons drifted over large regions of Arizona, New Mexico, and Texas, changing size and shape as they were buffeted by winds and heated by the sun. But Project Mogul remained so secret that even the scientists working on the mission did not know its code name.

"During the late 1940's and 1950's . . . the large, newly invented, polyethylene balloons . . . were often misidentified as flying saucers."[61]

—Air Force first lieutenant James McAndrew.

Whatever the top secret nature of Project Mogul, hundreds of spy balloons launched from Holloman crashed. On the rare occasions when they were discovered, as in Roswell, citizens were told the objects were simply weather balloons. Because of the classified nature of the payloads, areas where the balloons landed were cordoned off by military personnel. This aroused the suspicions of local officials and civilians. Senior SETI astronomer Seth Shostak provides perspective:

> In the beginning, they would've kept [the spy balloons] secret because they were trying to determine if the Soviet Union had the H-bomb. But the public finds it much more interesting to think that aliens traveled hundreds of light years, and in the last couple of hundred feet, made a navigational error and slammed into the New Mexico desert. . . .

It's more interesting to think that the government has the aliens freeze-dried and stacked up somewhere.[62]

The Roswellian Syndrome

The Roswell incident provided a basis for a condition called the Roswellian Syndrome by skeptics Joe Nickell and James Mc-Gaha. The Roswellian Syndrome is found in people who ignore realistic explanations for alleged alien visitations. The syndrome has four parts: a UFO-related event occurs, it is debunked by official sources, it is largely forgotten, and it is later revived as a conspiracy theory.

In Roswell, the crash of a mysterious aircraft briefly made headlines. The theory was quickly debunked when the Air Force

Stories of alien visitations on Earth continue to circulate despite efforts by credible sources to show that such events have not occurred—and it is likely that more such stories will continue to captivate humanity.

blamed a weather balloon for the debris. The case went underground for thirty-three years, completely out of the public view until *The Roswell Incident* was published in 1980. The book's publication launched a dozen conspiracy theories and countless copycat books, films, and television shows.

The Roswell incident and other alien stories seem to show that people prefer complicated accounts over straightforward explanations. While UFO skeptics provide seemingly obvious answers, believers describe childlike aliens, enemy invaders, and spaceships from other galaxies. When 80 percent of Americans think the government is conspiring to cover up the existence of aliens, there is a good chance that people will continue to spin complex tales of extraterrestrials. After all, these stories are much more interesting than the simple answers provided by experts.

Source Notes

Introduction: What Are Space Aliens?

1. Quoted in Ed Mazza, "NASA's Bold New NExSS Initiative Will Search for Signs of Life on Other Planets," *Huffington Post*, April 24, 2015. www.huffingtonpost.com.
2. Robert Todd Carroll, "Alien Abductions," Skeptic's Dictionary, September 12, 2015. http://skepdic.com.
3. Quoted in Mike Wall, "New Alien Life Claim Far from Convincing, Scientists Say," Space.com, September 12, 2013. www.space.com.

Chapter One: Why Do People Believe in Space Aliens?

4. Quoted in Christine A. Scheller, "NASA Astrobiologist Cites Three 'Clues' Consistent with Extraterrestrial Life," American Association for the Advancement of Science, October 11, 2013. www.aaas.org.
5. David A. Weintraub, *Religions and Extraterrestrial Life.* New York: Springer, 2014, p. 4.
6. Quoted in Weintraub, *Religions and Extraterrestrial Life*, p. 173.
7. Quoted in Weintraub, *Religions and Extraterrestrial Life*, p. 11.
8. Quoted in Weintraub, *Religions and Extraterrestrial Life*, p. 11.
9. Quoted in Michael J. Crowe, *The Extraterrestrial Life Debate, 1750–1900.* Cambridge, UK: Cambridge University Press, 1986, p. 11.

10. Quoted in Crowe, *The Extraterrestrial Life Debate*, p. 13.
11. Quoted in L.W. Labaree, ed., *Papers of Benjamin Franklin*, vol. 3. New Haven, CT: Yale University Press, 1959, p. 345.
12. Quoted in Crowe, *The Extraterrestrial Life Debate*, p. 128.
13. Quoted in Crowe, *The Extraterrestrial Life Debate*, p. 529.
14. Alfred Russel Wallace, *Is Mars Habitable?* New York: Macmillan, 1907, p. 20.
15. Carl Sagan, *Cosmos.* New York: Random House, 2002, p. 83.
16. H.G. Wells, *The War of the Worlds*, quoted at Fourmilab Switzerland, June 1995. www.fourmilab.ch.
17. Quoted in Annie Jacobsen, *Area 51: An Uncensored History of America's Top Secret Military Base.* New York: Little, Brown, 2011, p. 20.
18. Quoted in Jacobsen, *Area 51*, p. 21.
19. Quoted in Jacobsen, *Area 51*, p. 72.
20. Susan Sontag, "The Imagination of Disaster," *Commentary*, October 1, 1965. www.commentarymagazine.com.
21. Quoted in Lester D. Friedman and Brent Notbohm, *Steven Spielberg Interviews*. Jackson: University Press of Mississippi, 2000, pp. 31–32.
22. Quoted in Ray Villard, "Why Do People Believe in UFOs?," Discovery, August 10, 2012. http://news.discovery.com.
23. Villard, "Why Do People Believe in UFOs?"

Chapter Two: Encounters with Aliens

24. Quoted in Juju Chang and Jim Dubreuil, "Abducted by Aliens: Believers Tell Their Stories," ABC News, August 17, 2009. http://abcnews.go.com.
25. Quoted in Chang and Dubreuil, "Abducted by Aliens."
26. Quoted in Chang and Dubreuil, "Abducted by Aliens."
27. Quoted in Joanne Kimberlin, "Whatever Happened to the Ex-Marine Who Saw a UFO?," *Virginian-Pilot*, July 14, 2008. http://hamptonroads.com.
28. Quoted in Chang and Dubreuil, "Abducted by Aliens."
29. Quoted in Kimberlin, "Whatever Happened to the Ex-Marine Who Saw a UFO?"

30. Quoted in Oliver Darcy, "On Deathbed, Former 'Lockheed Martin Engineer' with 'Top Secret Clearance' Opens Up About . . . Aliens," *Blaze*, October 31, 2014. www.theblaze.com.

31. Quoted in Joshua Fechter, "Former Lockheed Martin Engineer from Texas: I Met Aliens at Area 51," MySA. www.mysanantonio.com.

32. Stuart J. Robbins, "Bushman's Deathbed Confessions," James Randi Educational Foundation, October 28, 2014. http://web.randi.org.

33. Quoted in Chang and Dubreuil, "Abducted by Aliens."

34. Richard J. McNally, "Explaining 'Memories' of Space Alien Abduction and Past Lives: An Experimental Psychopathology Approach," Harvard University, May 13, 2015. http://dash.harvard.edu.

35. McNally, "Explaining 'Memories' of Space Alien Abduction and Past Lives."

36. McNally, "Explaining 'Memories' of Space Alien Abduction and Past Lives."

37. Quoted in David J. Brown, "Alien Enlightenment: An Interview with John Mack," John E. Mack Institute, 2015. http://johnemackinstitute.org.

38. Joy S. Gilbert, "Joy S. Gilbert's Paranormal Experiences," Alien Contact & Human Evolution, 2012. http://aliencontactandhumanevolution.com.

39. Joy S. Gilbert, "Joy S. Gilbert, Contactee," Alien Contact & Human Evolution, 2012. http://aliencontactandhumanevolution.com.

40. Quoted in Brown, "Alien Enlightenment."

Chapter Three: The Search for Extraterrestrial Beings

41. Quoted in Irene Klotz, "2 New Exoplanets More Like Earth than Any Others," Discovery, January 6, 2015. http://news.discovery.com.

42. Deborah Byrd, "Is It True That Jupiter Protects Earth?," EarthSky, November 29, 2014. http://earthsky.org.

43. Quoted in ScienceDaily, "Earth-Sized Planets May Be Common Throughout Our Galaxy, NASA Survey Suggests," October 29, 2010. www.sciencedaily.com.

44. Quoted in Arthur C. Clarke Foundation, "Sir Arthur's Quotations," 2015. www.clarkefoundation.org.

45. Giuseppe Cocconi and Philip Morrison, "Searching for Interstellar Communications," Cosmic Search, September 21, 2004. www.bigear.org.

46. Quoted in F.D. Drake, "Project Ozma," *Physics Today*, April 1961, p. 40.

47. Quoted in Wilson de Silva, "Finding Aliens 'Only a Matter of Time,'" *Cosmos*, February 2010. www.wilsondasilva.com.

48. SETI Institute, "Fermi Paradox," 2015. www.seti.org.

49. Neil deGrasse Tyson, *Death by Black Hole.* New York: Norton, 2007, p. 235.

50. Quoted in Fay Schlesinger, "Stephen Hawking: Earth Could Be at Risk of an Invasion by Aliens Living in 'Massive Ships,'" *Daily Mail*, April 10, 2010. www.dailymail.co.uk.

51. Armando Azua-Bustos et al., "Regarding Messaging to Extraterrestrial Intelligence (METI)/Active Searches for Extraterrestrial Intelligence (Active SETI)," SETI@home, February 2015. http://setiathome.berkeley.edu.

52. Quoted in Seth Borenstein, "Dialing E.T., but Maybe Getting Klingons," *Toronto Star*, February 13, 2015. www.thestar.com.

53. Quoted in Borenstein, "Dialing E.T., but Maybe Getting Klingons."

Chapter Four: Are There Other Explanations for Space Aliens?

54. Quoted in Lindsay Deutsch, "UFO or CIA? Agency Takes Credit for '50s and '60s Sightings," *USA Today*, December 30, 2014. www.usatoday.com.

55. Quoted in Stanton T. Friedman and Don Berliner, *Crash at Corona*. New York: Paragon House, 1992, p. 73.

56. Quoted in Kal K. Korff, *The Roswell UFO Crash.* Amherst, NY: Prometheus, 1997, p. 28.

57. Quoted in Friedman and Berliner, *Crash at Corona*, p. 113.
58. Quoted in Nick Redfern, *Body Snatchers in the Desert.* New York: Paraview Pocket, 2005, p. 17.
59. Quoted in Michael Hesemann and Philip Mantle, *Beyond Roswell: The Alien Autopsy Film, Area 51 & the U.S. Government Coverup of UFOs.* London: O'Mara, 1997, pp. 39–40.
60. Donald Prothero, "Area 51, UFOs, Roswell, Commies, and Nazis—All Rolled into One Story!," *Skepticblog*, May 25, 2011. www.skepticblog.org.
61. James McAndrew, *The Roswell Report: Case Closed.* Washington, DC: US Government Printing Office, 1997, p. 41.
62. Quoted in Elliot Lee Speigel, "Roswell: Alien Spacecraft or Top Secret Spy Project?," ABC News, July 7, 2007. http://abcnews.go.com.

For Further Research

Books

Stanton T. Friedman, *UFOs: Real or Imagined? A Scientific Investigation*. New York: Rosen, 2011.

Richard Hammond, *Richard Hammond's Mysteries of the World: Alien Encounters*. London: Red Fox, 2015.

History Channel, *The Young Investigator's Guide to Ancient Aliens.* New York: Roaring Brook, 2015.

Ken Karst, *Area 51.* Mankato, MN: Creative Education, 2014.

Nick Redfern, *True Stories of Space Exploration Conspiracies.* New York: Rosen Classroom, 2014.

Nick Redfern, *True Stories of the Real Men in Black.* New York: Rosen Classroom, 2014.

Websites

Alien Contact & Human Evolution (http://aliencontactand humanevolution.com). This site is hosted by alien abductee Joy S. Gilbert, who maintains that she was enlightened by her numerous contacts with extraterrestrials over a period of twenty-two years. The site contains photos and videos of purported UFOs and aliens and essays on telepathy and other paranormal phenomena.

Exopolitics (http://exopolitics.org). This website was launched by Michael E. Salla in 2003 to publish purported evidence concerning the presence of extraterrestrials on Earth that had been covered up the US government. The site contains videos, articles, book reviews, and radio interviews.

James Randi Educational Foundation (http://web.randi.org). James Randi is a professional stage magician best known as an investigator and professional skeptic who once offered $1 million to anyone who could prove the existence of aliens. This website publishes articles and videos meant to debunk what it calls paranormal and pseudoscientific frauds in the media.

MUFON (www.mufon.com). Formerly the Midwest UFO Network, MUFON investigates UFO sightings and collects data to promote research and education about aliens, abductions, and alien spacecraft.

Reason.com (http://reason.com). The website for *Reason* magazine, which mostly focuses on politics and culture but also publishes articles relating to the paranormal, pseudoscience, and junk science.

SETI Institute (www.seti.org). The SETI Institute seeks evidence of life in the universe by looking for radio waves and other signals generated by alien technology. The website contains information about SETI projects, including the Alien Telescope Array, a large number of small radio telescopes designed to search millions of exoplanets for extraterrestrial intelligence.

Skeptic (www.skeptic.com). The website of the Skeptics Society, which uses science and reason to debunk UFO researchers, paranormal beliefs, fringe science, and extraordinary claims of all kinds.

Skeptic's Dictionary (http://skepdic.com). This site is hosted by Robert Todd Carroll, a philosophy professor and Committee for Skeptical Inquiry fellow. With alphabetical listings of articles ranging from abracadabra to zombies, Carroll provides in-depth descriptions of paranormal subjects, skeptical commentary, and explanations of why people believe what they do.

UFO Digest (http://ufodigest.com). This website provides updates concerning the latest UFO sightings and features blogs, books, film reviews, conspiracy theories, and information concerning aliens and beings such as vampires, angels, and werewolves.

Index

Picture Credits

About the Author

Stuart A. Kallen is the author of more than three hundred nonfiction books for children and young adults. He has written on topics ranging from the theory of relativity to the art of animation. In addition, Kallen has written award-winning children's videos and television scripts. In his spare time, he is a singer/songwriter/guitarist in San Diego.